THE
BLURRY
RULES
BOOK

it's a God thing!

Other Books Available

The Lily Series

Here's Lily!
Lily Robbins, M.D. (Medical Dabbler)
Lily and the Creep
Lily's Ultimate Party
Ask Lily
Lily the Rebel
Lights, Action, Lily!
Lily Rules!
Rough & Rugged Lily
Lily Speaks!
Horse Crazy Lily
Lily's Church Camp Adventure
Lily's Passport to Paris
Lily's in London?!

Nonfiction

The Beauty Book
The Body Book
The Buddy Book
The Best Bash Book
The Blurry Rules Book
The It's MY Life Book
The Creativity Book
The Uniquely Me Book
The Year 'Round Holiday Book
The Values & Virtues Book
The Fun-Finder Book
The Walk-the-Walk Book
Dear Diary
Girlz Want to Know
NIV Young Women of Faith Bible
YWOF Journal: Hey! This Is Me
Take It from Me

THE BLURRY RULES BOOK

it's a God thing!

Written by Nancy Rue
Illustrated by Lyn Boyer

Zonderkidz

Zonder**kidz**®

The children's group of Zondervan

The Blurry Rules Book
Copyright © 2001 by Women of Faith
Illustrations copyright © 2001 by Lyn Boyer

Requests for information should be addressed to:
Grand Rapids, Michigan 49530

ISBN: 0–310–70152–X

Published in association with the literary agency of Alive Communications, Inc., 7680 Goddard Street, Suite 200, Colorado Springs, CO 80920.

Art direction and interior design by Michelle Lenger

Printed in the United States of America

04 05 06 07 /❖ DC/ 13 12 11 10 9 8 7 6 5

Contents

Who's Number One?

**I am the Lord your God ... You shall
have no other gods before me.**
Exodus 20:2–3

Is it just me, or did Moses make it sound really easy when he came down from Mt. Sinai with the Ten Commandments and said, "This is what we have to do to obey God"? How tough is it not to make idols, steal, kill, cheat, swear, and lie about people? To hear him tell it, being obedient is a piece of cake.

But if you live past the age of about two, you figure out that it's harder than it sounds! The Girlz certainly have realized it.

Lily wouldn't *dream* of committing murder. But when Shad Shifferdecker announces in the cafeteria—in a voice loud enough for the whole *world* to hear—that Lily is pigeon-toed, Lily wouldn't mind *too much* if Shad were suddenly stricken with "terminal" appendicitis. Yet isn't wishing somebody would drop dead about as bad as holding a gun on them?

Reni *knows* that cheating is wrong. But during a science test when she sees one of her friends glancing at someone else's paper before writing down an answer, she has a tough decision to make. Can *not* reporting someone else for cheating be anywhere near as bad as, say, copying someone else's term paper?

You don't have to tell Zooey it's *wrong* to say something about somebody that isn't true. Still, when Chelsea and Ashley—*the* two most popular girls in the whole class—are discussing Marcie McCleary with her, what's so terrible about saying something not-so-nice about Marcie (provided that it's true, of course)? After all, it isn't every day that Chelsea and Ashley even *look* at Zooey, much less *talk* to her.

When you get right down to it, following the Ten Commandments—God's guides for right living—isn't that easy. Just like Lily and her friends, you're bound to face plenty of situations where the rules aren't spelled out all that clearly. What do you do then?

What if your life is so crowded you don't have time to pray and read your Bible—but you keep hearing that you're supposed to put God before everything else?

What if all—and I mean *all*—your friends are getting their noses pierced, and you're going to feel like a complete loser if you don't do it too—but you're pretty sure you've heard in church that it's *God* you're supposed to be worshiping?

What if keeping the Sabbath day holy means sitting through a really boring Sunday school class and an even worse worship service?

What if those parents you're supposed to be honoring do stuff that's *so* unfair?

What if your friend's wardrobe, that you're not supposed to covet, is calling your name? What if—

You get the idea. When it gets down to the nitty-gritty, those kinds of decisions can be difficult, and rules like "Thou shalt not kill" don't really seem to apply. But not to worry—God has it all covered, and this book is in your hands to help you figure out how. There isn't a situation you could possibly face that the Father doesn't have a solution for. It may not be as easy as Moses made it sound, but it isn't impossible. The bugaboos of life can be conquered!

HOW IS THIS A God Thing?

You aren't the first one to ask "What if?" Back when Jesus was here on earth, people asked him questions like that all the time.

"What if I divorce my wife, only I do it legally? Isn't that okay?"

"What if somebody hits me first? Don't I have the right to hit them back?"

"What if some out-of-it person wants to hang out with me? Isn't that bad for my reputation?"

"What if I've given all my money to the church? Do I still have to take care of my parents in their old age?"

"What if my brother or sister hurts me? How many times do I have to forgive?"

"What if I'm really rich—do I have to give up *everything* to follow you?"

"What if I promise something, only I have my fingers crossed? Does it still count? Isn't a promise only a promise if I have my hand on the Bible?"

Never once did Jesus say, "Gosh, I don't know. Let me get back to you on that." He always had guidelines to share, and they all boiled down to basically two things:

Does what you want to do show that you love God with all your heart, body, and mind (which pretty much covers everything!)? (Matthew 22:37)

AND

Does what you want to do show that you love your neighbor the way you do yourself? (Matthew 22:39)

As we look at some of the not-so-easy decisions you have to make, we'll come back to those two guidelines from Jesus again and again and show exactly how they work.

They're what we call a **frame of reference**. It's sort of like when you get separated from your mom or your friends at the mall and you start to feel a little lost and uneasy. If you can spot that huge piece of art in the center of the mall, you can always figure out where you are "in reference" to that. It's like a land-mark that guides you. Jesus' two greatest commandments are like landmarks too.

Think of the Ten Commandments as the mall itself. If you want to get around in there and find what you need, you constantly have to look back at what Jesus says about loving God and loving your neighbor as yourself. Those two principles serve as a **frame of reference** for your life just like the huge piece of art serves as a **frame of reference** for the mall.

So let's start with the first of God's rules that Moses brought down from the mountain:

I am the LORD your God, who brought you out of Egypt,
out of the land of slavery. You shall have no other gods before me.
Exodus 20:2–3

Simple enough, right? No pushing God out of the way for any of those ridiculous-looking idols.

Let's find out—

CHECK **Yourself** OUT

If you're ready to be *really* honest with yourself, find a spot where you can be all alone for a few minutes, where nobody is going to be looking over your shoulder. Then, number the items on the list below in order of how important they are to you. Number one will be the most important, number two the second most important, and so on.

If you have trouble deciding, ask yourself this question: which one of these things would I have the most trouble giving up? That would be number one. The one you'd have *almost* as much trouble letting go of would be number two. Be sure to think about the *consequences* of giving up certain things, as well as how you feel about those activities! Okay, here we go:

_____ the time I spend with my parents

_____ the time I spend hanging out with my friends

_____ the time I spend doing things I enjoy by myself

_____ the time I spend with God

_____ the time I spend taking lessons or doing sports

_____ the time I spend with my brothers and sisters

_____ the time I spend doing homework and studying

_____ the time I spend doing chores

What you've just done is **prioritize** the activities in your life. That means you've decided the order of their importance to you. If you marked "the time I spend hanging out with my friends" number one,

that means being with them, doing stuff like watching movies and consuming large quantities of microwave popcorn, is the most important thing in your life. If you marked "the time I spend doing chores" number one, that means the most important thing in your life is doing chores. (It could also mean that you need a brain transplant!)

So what's the right answer?

Let's get back to our **frame of reference**. If you go by our first commandment (love God with all your heart, body, and mind), then your number one choice *should* be "the time I spend with God."

I can see you now, grabbing your eraser to fix that on your quiz and saying, "I knew that—I did! I *meant* to make that number one!" But don't feel bad. It's really difficult in today's busy world to put the right things first. You aren't the only one.

Girlz WANT TO KNOW

✿ **LILY:** *By the time I go to school all day, then have a Girlz Only Club meeting, then go home and set the table, have dinner, help with the dishes, do my homework, talk to some of my friends on the phone, take a bath, brush my teeth, write in my journal, and fight with my little brother, I have about five minutes left to pray before I fall asleep!*

✿ **RENI:** *I'm in the school orchestra, and I'm taking private violin lessons. My parents say I have a gift from God for music and they're proud of me for using it. Isn't that putting God first?*

✿ **ZOOEY:** *Yikes! My mom doesn't even take me to church. I didn't know you were supposed to spend time with God. How do you do that anyway?*

✿ **KRESHA:** *If I try to have quiet time with God, my brothers are going to make fun of me—I know it. I'll have to hide in the closet or something! Is that really what God wants?*

✿ **SUZY:** *I thought God was just with me all the time. How can I spend more time with him than that?*

If you have questions like these, you may need to find some new ways to organize the time you don't spend in school, sleeping, or doing other necessary things so that you can have some special time just for God. As we go along, you'll learn more about what to do with that time once you've found it.

Just Do It

Time never stops. It never slows down, and it never speeds up. Everybody, from the president of the United States to your baby brother, gets the same number of seconds, minutes, and hours every day, and everyone gets the same number of days, weeks, and months in every year. If *anybody* can find a way to get it all in, including quiet time with God, *everybody* can. Let's take a look at how.

Start by filling in this chart with your activities for the last couple of days. Write a few words about how you spent each period of time. For instance, from midnight to 6:00 A.M. on the first day, you were probably sleeping, so write "sleeping" in each box for that time period. Maybe from 6:00 to 9:00 P.M. last night you were watching television, so write "watching television" in each box for that time period.

Time	Ⓐ Day Before Yesterday	Ⓑ Yesterday	Ⓒ Today
Midnight–1:00 A.M.			
1:00–2:00 A.M.			
2:00–3:00 A.M.			
3:00–4:00 A.M.			
4:00–5:00 A.M.			
5:00–6:00 A.M.			
6:00–7:00 A.M.			
7:00–8:00 A.M.			
8:00–9:00 A.M.			
9:00–10:00 A.M.			

10:00–11:00 A.M.		
11:00–Noon		
12:00–1:00 P.M.		
1:00–2:00 P.M.		
2:00–3:00 P.M.		
3:00–4:00 P.M.		
4:00–5:00 P.M.		
5:00–6:00 P.M.		
6:00–7:00 P.M.		
7:00–8:00 P.M.		
8:00–9:00 P.M.		
9:00–10:00 P.M.		
10:00–11:00 P.M.		
11:00–Midnight		

Now fill out the next chart. List in the column headed "Activity" each thing you did during the last three days, such as sleeping, doing homework, watching television, playing computer games, or doing chores. Under "Total Hours Spent Each Day," add up how much time you spent doing each activity each of the three days. Then add up the total hours you spent on each activity the whole three days and fill in the total in the last column.

Activity	Total Hours Spent Each Day	Total
Ⓐ		
Ⓑ		
Ⓒ		

Okay, now ask yourself these questions:

14

What did I spend the most time doing BESIDES sleeping and going to school?

What did I spend the least time doing?

What would I like to have spent more time doing?

What would I like to have spent less time doing (besides sleeping and going to school!)?

What would I like to have done but didn't do at all?

Did I have enough free time when I could do whatever I wanted?

Did I get to decide when I wanted to do things at least some of the time?

Do I like the way I spent the time I had control over (the time when I wasn't asleep or at school)?

Believe it or not, you really do have the power to plan what you do with some of your time, and it can actually be fun. If this sounds like *your* kind of fun, you'll need:

- a large sheet of poster paper.
- a calendar with spaces big enough to write in for each day.
- a pencil with an eraser.
- a pad of paper.

Before you start, remember these things:

First, you don't have to make plans for everything you do every day, because you do some things automatically, like getting dressed, eating, going to school, taking a bath, and sleeping. You should allow time for those things, but you don't have to make special plans to do them.

Second, even though you're young—like maybe not even in middle school yet—you can still make some plans for the **whole year** ahead. That may sound kind of scary, but actually it's exciting!

Step 1

Look at the answers to the questions under "Check Yourself Out." Use them to help you decide these things: What do I want to do this year? Do I want to obtain something? Become something? Learn something? Make something? Go someplace? Get to know someone? If you really want to make spending time with God the most important thing in your life, this is the place to include that: *I want to get into the habit of spending special time with God every day.*

Step 2

Write down the answers to those questions in Step 1 in the form of a list on your pad of paper. These examples may help you:

Lily's List

- Find a way to spend quiet time with God every day.
- Write for the school newspaper.

- Make straight A's.
- Learn how to French braid my hair.
- Learn how to speak French.
- Take Otto to obedience school.

Reni's List

- Buy a violin of my own instead of renting one.
- Be able to play "The Flight of the Bumble Bee."
- Go to orchestra camp.
- Make citywide middle-school orchestra.
- Meet a professional violinist.
- Spend quiet time with God

Zooey's List

- Lose fifty pounds.
- Make good grades so I can be in honors classes in eighth grade.
- Redecorate my bedroom.
- Go away to summer camp.
- Join a church.

Kresha's List

- Learn to speak English really well.
- Get a new hairstyle.
- Try out for the soccer team.
- Try out for the softball team.
- Try out for the cheerleading squad.
- Find a husband for my mom.
- Have that quiet time thing with God.

Suzy's List

- Stop being so shy.
- Get along better with my sister.
- Read the whole Bible.
- Go to a better soccer camp next summer.
- Learn to do a double back flip.

Step 3

Cross out the things that are impossible—just *ain't* gonna happen—or that really aren't that important to you after all. Get rid of the things that, on second thought, you don't really want to do or won't be able to do. You can also change things a little instead of crossing them out.

Lily realized she wouldn't be able to learn to speak fluent French in a year, so she changed her goal to taking a French class. She also remembered that her hair is pretty wild and thick and decided that trying to learn to French braid it might be a lost cause. She crossed that out.

Reni remembered that she's just a beginner and "The Flight of the Bumble Bee" is for advanced students, so she crossed that out. And since chances are she won't get to meet a professional violinist, she crossed that out too. Then she took getting her own violin off the list, because her parents are going to send her to orchestra camp. She realized they probably couldn't afford both.

Zooey decided that fifty pounds might be a little ambitious, so she changed her goal to ten pounds. She felt that was plenty to get started. Then she decided to work hard to make the best grades she can and not worry about whether that puts her in honors classes.

Kresha, after thinking about it, decided she'd better let her mom find her own husband when she's ready. She crossed that out, along with being on the softball team and cheerleading squad. She knew that time wouldn't allow her to be involved in *all* the sports that interest her, so she decided to focus on her favorite—soccer.

Suzy decided that reading the *whole* Bible might be too much, but thought she could read the four Gospels in a year. And forget the double back flip—too dangerous, and once she decided to concentrate on soccer rather than gymnastics, she didn't need it anyway.

Step 4

Make a priority list. Remember that word *prioritize?* Decide which of the things still left on your list are most important, which are not quite as important, and which are least important.

Number the things on your list, putting the most important things at the top of the pad of paper, the least important things at the bottom, and the other things in the middle. Here's what Lily's list looks like now:

1. Find a way to spend quiet time with God every day.
2. Make straight A's.
3. Write for the school newspaper.
4. Take Otto to obedience school.
5. Take a French class.

Step 5

Write your list on the poster paper and put it up where you can see it every day. Decorate it so that it's fun to look at as you're being reminded of the things you want to accomplish during the year. These are your **goals.**

Now that you have a plan for the whole year, you're ready to move on to **monthly and weekly plans**. Remember: A lot of what you do during a month or a week will depend on your goals for the year.

Step 6

Write your first goal from your yearly list at the top of a piece of paper on your pad. Below it, write down everything you can think of that you need to do to reach your goal.

Lily's List

Goal: Find a way to spend quiet time with God every day.

• Decide on a good time.
• Ask Mom to make Joe leave me alone.

- Get a journal.
- Find a devotional guide I can follow.
- Get a Bible I can understand!
- Ask my youth pastor about the best way to pray.
- Pray about it.

Step 7

Number the items on the list in the order in which you'll need to do them. That will take some thought and maybe even the help of someone who understands your goal. Look at Lily's revised list below. If *spending time with God every day* is your goal, feel free to copy this list and use it as your own. It's a great way to achieve that goal and obey that first commandment to the letter!

Lily's List

Goal: Find a way to spend quiet time with God every day.

1. *Pray about it.* That makes sense, doesn't it? God wants to talk to you about the time you'll be spending together. If you simply tell God what you want to accomplish and ask for his help, things will fall together much more smoothly.

2. *Ask my youth pastor about the best way to pray.* If you don't have a youth pastor, go to someone who knows and likes kids your age. It should be someone you admire as a Christian. Such a person will almost certainly be excited to share ideas with you. If there's absolutely no one you can go to, simply talk to God in whatever way seems comfortable. There is no "right" or "wrong" way to pray. God loves you and wants to hear what you have to say.

3. *Find a devotional guide I can follow.* There's so much to deal with when you're getting close to God—like, for instance, where to start? A devotional guide written for someone your age can be very helpful. It will suggest things for you to think and pray about. It will direct you to specific passages in the Bible that will make those things even clearer. The Bible is, after all, one of the ways God speaks to us. There is a

special devotional guide made for Young Women of Faith like you called *Dear Diary*. But there are tons more in Christian bookstores and your church library. Your pastor, your mom, or some of your Christian friends can help you find what you need.

4. *Purchase a journal and a Bible I can understand.* (A little shopping excursion is in order!) It's good to have some sort of blank book for writing down thoughts, prayers, questions, and discoveries. You can even draw pictures of what you're thinking. Bookstores and gift shops have them, or you can make your own out of a notebook. A Bible translated into simpler, more understandable language is also a big help. If you're going to get a new one, go to your Christian bookstore and look through the various versions until you find one that's easy for you to read. If you have to make do with what's around the house, don't be afraid to make a list of questions about things you don't understand and ask someone about them when your quiet time is over.

5. *Decide on a good time.* Look over your daily activities and locate a block of time, at least thirty minutes, when you can be completely alone without interruptions. Can you get up a half hour earlier in the morning—which might mean going to bed a half hour earlier? Do you concentrate better in the evening? If that's the case, can you give up a half hour of television or computer time—or phone time—to spend with God before you go to bed? Once you choose a time, treat that commitment with the same respect you would give to a dental appointment or a piano lesson. Nothing short of an emergency should keep you away. (Remember: You've promised God you'll be there!)

6. *Ask Mom to make Joe leave me alone.* It's really important to let your family and friends know when and where you're going to have your quiet time each day. Make sure you're not stepping into someone else's space and time, and then ask everyone to respect yours as well. If there's someone especially troublesome—like a curious little sister or a brother who likes to tease—ask for Mom's and Dad's support rather than taking matters into your own hands! (That isn't tattling—that's just smart!)

Step 8

Take out your calendar and turn to this month. In the little squares, write the things you already have scheduled. Include the following:

- • Things you've promised to do with other people—like parties, sleepovers, taking your little sister to the movies, special church activities
- Regular activities besides school—like ballet classes, soccer practices, piano lessons
- Appointments that have been made for you—like going to the dentist, seeing the orthodontist, getting your hair cut

Step 9

Now that you can see where your empty spaces are, fill in exactly when you want to do the things on your list from step seven. Lily's calendar looks like this:

Sunday	Monday	Tuesday	Wednesday	Thursday	Friday	Saturday
Sunday	Monday	Tuesday	Wednesday	Thursday	Friday	Saturday
Sunday	Monday	Tuesday	Wednesday	Thursday	Friday	Saturday
Sunday	Monday	Tuesday	Wednesday	Thursday	Friday	Saturday

You can now go back and repeat steps seven, eight, and nine for the other goals on your poster-chart, except that you'll turn to a new month for each one. Some goals may take longer than a month to achieve, and if that becomes hard for you to figure out, get someone (like your mom) to help you.

Step 10

That pretty much sets you up for the year, the month, and maybe even the week! Now you can make your **daily** plans. Here's an easy way to do it:

- Keep that pad of paper and pencil nearby.
- Whenever you think of something you need to get done or want to do, write it down on your pad. Lily's list looks like this right now, although it changes every day, as you'll see.

Stuff I Have to Do

1. Return library books.
2. Get field trip permission slip signed.
3. Give Otto a bath.
4. Make a birthday card for Joe.

Each morning before you start your day, look at your calendar and add the things in the square to your "STUFF I HAVE TO DO" list. Now Lily's list looks like this:

Stuff I Have to Do (Revised)

1. Return library books.
2. Get field trip permission slip signed.
3. Give Otto a bath.
4. Make birthday card for Joe.
5. Call Pastor Michael to see when I can talk to him about praying and stuff.

If there's something you're trying to develop into a daily habit, write it down on your list *every* day until it becomes so natural you don't have to remind yourself to do it anymore.

Lily will add another point to her to do list:

6. Pray about having quiet time.

Lily doesn't have everything "set up" yet for regular quiet time, but she doesn't have to have everything just right before she can begin. She can spend a half hour before bed just talking to God, writing her prayers in the "Talking to God about It" section of this book, even writing down questions she wants to talk to him about. God just wants her full attention for that time—and yours.

Keep your list in your backpack, pocket, or purse so you can remember to do stuff. It's also fun to cross off things as you do them—and you can make it even *more* fun by using colored markers or pencils or drawing smiley faces or giving yourself stickers for things you've accomplished. The more you enjoy your list, the more often you'll use it.

At the end of the day, check your "STUFF I HAVE TO DO" list. If there's something you haven't crossed off, put it at the top of your list for the next day. After all, unexpected things *do* come up that might keep you from getting things done from time to time. This way, you won't lose track of them.

You may be thinking: *What if I do all this planning, but I can't get myself to actually do the stuff?*

That's a *very* human question. Don't let it cause you to give up before you even start! You *can* learn to follow through and make progress on your goals. Let's look at how.

Girlz WANT TO KNOW

✿ *LILY: I get this great list all organized and I do most of the stuff— but then sometimes I get to something I just don't want to do and I talk myself out of it. How can I quit doing that?*

Ah, **procrastination!** That's something we're all guilty of now and then. One way to beat procrastination—after praying about it first, because God *will* help you with it—is to do the things you don't want to do first, before you do any of the fun stuff on your list. It's so much easier to do the yucky duties when you're rested and fresh, before you have a chance to tell yourself you're just too tired to do them.

❀ *RENI: I tried the list thing, but there was so much stuff on it, I got freaked out and just turned on the television.*

There are two problems here, Reni. Problem number one is **overloading**. Try not to put more than one job per hour on your list. If you have two free hours after school, put only two jobs or activities on your pad for that time. If you have extra time, then you can always add things. (It's fun to put something down on your list that wasn't there at first, just so you can cross it off!) If doing only one thing an hour puts you too far behind, talk to your mom and dad about your scheduling problem. You may be involved in too many things and need to uncrowd your life a little.
If you don't deal with overload, you almost certainly will be tempted to **escape** (problem number two) your responsibilities—and the ways to do that are endless! Watching television, reading, daydreaming, talking on the phone, goofing around, playing video games—those things aren't bad in themselves. You actually need a little down time like that every day. The problem comes in when you do *those* things and none of the things you *planned* to do. Here's where prayer is really helpful. Ask God to help you have the discipline and the energy to do what needs to be done. Imagine yourself doing those things. Imagine how bummed out you're going to feel if you don't do them. Talking to God about it *does* help—because you can't escape from God!

❀ *ZOOEY: I tell my mom I'm going to start my homework as soon as I get home from school. All the way home on the bus, I promise myself that I'm going to do just that. But if Mom isn't there when I get home, I always end up calling my friends or making nachos or something.*

That's one of the most important bugaboos to swat down, Zooey. What's happening is that you're **deceiving** your mom and yourself by not following through on what you say you're going to do. It will make your mom lose her trust in you—and after a while you won't trust yourself, either.

Ask your mom to **hold you accountable.** That means tell her what you're trying to do and ask her to check in to make sure you're doing it—in an encouraging rather than a punishing or critical way. Don't hesitate to ask her to give you a pep talk if you need one, and when she gets home, ask her to check your work. Knowing someone else is counting on you will help you learn to count on yourself.

✿ *SUZY: I don't have any trouble doing the things on my list that I like to do, like working on my soccer plays so I can get into a better camp next summer. But things like cleaning out my closet or writing thank-you notes—I can put that stuff off forever!*

Hey, Suzy, how about turning the not-so-fun stuff into a game? Set the timer and see if you can get the job done before it dings. If the task is something you have to do every week or every day, try to beat last week's or yesterday's time. A little challenge makes boring tasks more interesting.

✿ *KRESHA: I don't get allowance or even a "good job" from my mom for doing chores or homework. Sometimes that makes me feel like "Who cares?"*

When you set goals for yourself and achieve them, that makes you feel good. When someone else sets them, there's no guarantee that you're going to get that same good feeling! There are two things you can try. First, turn those un-fun jobs into *your* goals: *I will become a more helpful person* or *I will come up one letter grade in math during this next six weeks.* That way when you take those little steps, it feels good to you. Second, reward yourself for doing those things, even if nobody else does. *As soon as I finish these dishes,* you might promise yourself, *I'm going to have some cookies and listen to my new CD.* After a while, those jobs will become part of your day and you won't have to reward yourself every time you do them—although once in a while, we can all use a treat!

Talking to God About It

Remember that no matter how many lists or promises or calendars you make, you won't be able to succeed in any of it if you don't have God's help. You absolutely, positively can't do it alone. Nobody can! So start right now. Maybe this will help you get started.

Dear _____ (your favorite way of addressing our Lord),

I have some goals I want to accomplish. Could you help me know, first of all, if they're the ones you want me to work on? Especially this one: _____. Would you help me to look all around me for the answers? Will you help me to trust you?

And, God, would you please be there in the planning? Will you help me to make good decisions, especially about
_____?

I know I have trouble with some things, Lord, so would you also make me strong and wise and disciplined when it comes to these?
_____ Procrastination
_____ Overloading myself
_____ Escaping my responsibilities
_____ Not keeping my promises
Will you help me to do whatever it takes to stay on track?
_____ Doing the yucky stuff first
_____ Making up games
_____ Rewarding myself or anything else you might have in mind for me.

Most of all, I'm asking you to help me make my time with you the most important thing on my list. Please don't let me forget that or give up on it, and when I do, please forgive me and bring me back. I love you!

You've been working hard. Let's play! Think of one really big dream goal that you would absolutely *love* to reach. No matter how unrealistic it may seem, dream about it.

Write out just exactly how you'd go about achieving it.

I'm Not Worthy!

**You shall not make for yourself an idol . . .
You shall not bow down to them
or worship them.**

Exodus 20:4–5

Me? Bow Down?

We're going to look at three questions in this chapter.

1. How do I make choices?
2. How do I spend my money?
3. How do I worship God?

These three questions may not seem to go together, but they do—because all three have to do with the second of the Ten Commandments: "You shall not make for yourself an idol. . . . You shall not bow down to them or worship them" (Exodus 20:4-5) Answering these questions will help you identify what idols you bow down to.

"But I don't worship *any* idols!" you may be saying indignantly. Okay, you may not throw yourself down in front of a statue, but let's look at some things you might be "worshiping" without even realizing it.

Circle the answer under each statement that fits you best:

1. When a new fashion or fad comes out

  _____ a. I kind of ignore it.
  _____ b. I usually get in on it eventually—or at least I want to!
  _____ c. I'm the first one to get it.

2. If my two best friends started wearing a style that looked stupid on me, I would

  _____ a. not wear it even if they begged me to.
  _____ b. at least think about doing it because—well, they're my friends.
  _____ c. wear it no matter how dumb I looked.

3. I have bought or asked somebody to buy me something I've seen advertised on television

  _____ a. almost never.

_____ b. several times.

_____ c. all the time.

4. If I have a problem, the first one I tell is

    _____ a. God.

    _____ b. my mom or dad or some other adult.

    _____ c. one of my friends or siblings.

5. The words to the music I like to listen to most

    _____ a. are about God and other things that make me feel "lifted up."

    _____ b. aren't important to me one way or the other; I just listen to what everybody listens to.

    _____ c. are about things my parents wouldn't really approve of; I have to keep it turned way down.

6. If I had a chance to earn $25 on a Sunday evening, I would

    _____ a. pass it up because I never miss church/youth group on Sunday nights.

    _____ b. do it because I don't usually go to church or youth group on Sunday nights anyway.

    _____ c. do it even though I usually go to church/youth group on Sunday nights.

7. When I'm with my friends I

    _____ a. just act like myself—who else would I be?

    _____ b. try to act the way they're acting if I start feeling awkward or funky.

    _____ c. act the way they do all the time—even if it's not always how I feel like acting.

8. I worship God by

    _____ a. going to church and participating by singing and joining in the prayers. I get into it!

    _____ b. going to church—although I get bored sometimes.

_____ c. uh . . . am I supposed to worship God?

Now count up your a's, b's, and c's:

_____ a's   _____ b's   _____ c's

Let's see what your answers tell about how you make your decisions:

If you had more a's than you did other letters, that usually means you make your decisions based on what *you* think, what you know is right—and you know what's right because you know God. You're in a good place! Keep reading, though, because it's so easy to fall into other decision-making habits. You'll want to know what to watch out for.

If you had more b's than other letters, it indicates that you often go along with what other people do even when it isn't necessarily what you want to do or think you should do. That may be because you haven't really connected with God yet. If you read this chapter and do the activities, you will see yourself growing stronger and starting to have more of a mind of your own—the mind God gives you.

If you had more c's than other letters, other things—like friends, advertising, money—are probably making your choices for you. You might not feel very at ease a lot of the time because you're not doing it your way—and God's way. Definitely read on in this chapter and do the activities. You should begin to see a difference in the way you make decisions—a difference that's sure to make you happier.

HOW IS THIS A **God Thing?**

Number two on Moses' big list is: "You shall not make for yourself an idol. . . . You shall not bow down to them or worship them."

That sounds pretty simple. I mean, really, when was the last time you made another god for yourself and started praying to it? But Jesus reminds us that we can do that without even realizing we're doing it:

"Do not store up for yourselves treasures on earth,
where moth and rust destroy, and where thieves break in and steal.
But store up for yourselves treasures in heaven. . . .

For where your treasure is, there your heart will be also."
Matthew 6:19–21

"No one can serve two masters. Either he will hate the one and love the other, or he will be devoted to the one and despise the other. You cannot serve both God and Money."
Matthew 6:24

"It is easier for a camel to go through the eye of a needle than for a rich man to enter the kingdom of God."
Matthew 19:24

Is Jesus saying some of these things to you? Is it possible that he's saying:

- "Why do you beg and whine and drive your parents nuts to get you every new style or fad or trend that comes along? *I* am what makes you acceptable, not your hipness to the latest thing."
- "Why are you wearing clothes and doing things you don't even enjoy just so you can be like your friends? *I* am what makes you lovable, not your clone-buddies."
- "Why do you let people you don't even know tell you from inside a television set who you ought to be? *I* am what makes you special, not that girl in the ad."
- "Why do you take your problems to people who don't know any more about life than you do? Why don't you ever come to me? *I* am your comforter and your counselor, and I guide your parents and other wise people to help you."
- "Why do you listen to music that puts bad ideas into the beautiful mind the Father gave you? The Father meant for music to be a gift to lift you up, not drag you down."
- "Why is money more important to you than just about anything else? Why do you constantly want people to buy things for you? *I* will provide everything you really need."
- "Why do you try to act like somebody else? *I* can help you lose your false self that is trying to imitate other people and help you find out who you really are."

Circle the points where Jesus seems to be talking to you. Those are the things you'll want to pay special attention to as you read on.

Girlz WANT TO KNOW

So what do we *do* to stop "bowing down" to stuff that isn't God?

✿   *LILY: Okay, you can say, "Worship God and not new clothes," and I agree with that. But when I'm totally out of style and other girls are saying rude things to me and about me, I feel like a geek. Then I get all cranky and upset and I can't think about God anyway! What can I do about that?*

It's hard, isn't it? One of the reasons everybody doesn't worship God before absolutely everything else is because it isn't easy to do. That's the first thing. The second thing is, it isn't really the clothes, the fashions, the trends that you may be worshiping, it's other people's opinions of you. It isn't a bad thing to dress stylishly—it's only bad to do it just so other people will accept you.

If you can't afford some trendy purchase, or it's a pretty good bet the item will be out of style in a couple of weeks, or you really don't like the new fashion all that much, or the money could be used for something else you really like or need more—*but* you go with the trend and buy it anyway— that's worshiping it. So no one's asking you to dress like you're growing up in the '50s! Just check your reasons for having to be up to the minute before you head for the mall.

✿   *RENI: I am so into playing the violin now I can't even tell you. I'd rather go to my lesson or practice with the orchestra than, like, eat! Does that mean I'm worshiping it?*

No, not unless you're practicing on Sunday morning instead of going to church or thinking your gift for music is all because of *you*. If you're making choices based on your need to succeed as a violinist rather than on what you know God wants for your life, you're worshiping it. For example, do you secretly hope that another good player in your class messes up on her next test so you can take her place as first chair? If so, you're letting your desire to be seen as the "best" influence you more than what God would have you do, which is pray that she'll do her best. You don't have to give up playing the violin—you just have to change the way you think about it. God will help you do that if you ask him.

❀ *SUZY: I get five dollars a week allowance for doing my chores. Out of that I have to buy any snacks I want besides what my mom packs for me, pay my way into movies or the skating rink with my friends, and save for bigger stuff I want, like a new soccer ball. I know I'm supposed to give 10 percent of that back to the church, but that's fifty cents a week—two dollars a month. By the time I do all that other stuff, it just seems like a lot. Would I be worshiping money if I gave less? What's two dollars to my big church anyway?*

Let's take your last question first: What's that little bit of money to a big church? The point really isn't what your money does for the church, it's what the act of giving it does for you. It reminds you to depend on God rather than on money, and it shows that you trust him when he says to give 10 percent of all that you have (which is called **tithing**), and he will make sure you have enough for the rest of your needs. Of course, that doesn't cover your *wants*—things like snacks, movies, or that new soccer ball. If you are content with getting just what you *need*, God will make sure you get some treats now and then. That's the kind of God he is. When you decide not to give the 10 percent God asks because you want to make sure you get what you want, you're definitely trusting money more than God, and you're worshiping what it can buy. Faithfully give your 10 percent tithe for the next month and watch what happens. I'm willing to bet you won't go without much that you genuinely want.

The key to all of this—to your attitude about money, to the way you deal with fads and trends, to all of the decisions you make—is whether you're making a God-choice or a You-choice. You'll know that you're growing spiritually when the two are the same!

You may be asking, "Sure, but how do I do that?" The answer: you make room for God so that he takes up most of the space in you—more than your friends' opinions, more than what's popular, more than your thoughts about money and what it can buy.

Just Do It

Let's work on making room for God. You won't be able to do all of these things right away. You'll want to take them one at a time, work on each one, and probably keep working on them all your life! This is just to give you a start. You might even take them one by one and put them on your calendar and on your "Stuff I Have to Do" list.

Now, got that pad of paper and pencil ready again?

- Make a list of the people you choose to spend time with—not the people who live in your house or sit around you in your classroom, but the ones you have choices about. Look at your list. Think and pray about each person. Is this someone who makes fun of you because you go to church and believe in Christ? Does this person put you down and make you feel icky about yourself? Does this person try to talk you into doing stuff you know isn't right? Does this individual show disrespect for the things you respect, like parents, good teachers, the law, and God? Though it may be difficult, you ought to consider not hanging around with anyone who does one or more of those things. He or she is taking up room you need for God. People who admire your faith, allow you to feel good about yourself and share your conviction about the right way to live don't try to push God out. Instead they encourage you to make even more room for God in your life.
- Make a list of your favorite television shows, songs, and movies. Add what magazines and books you like to read. Look at your list and think and pray about each item. Do any of these talk about things your parents would flip out over? Do any of them talk about things you wouldn't bring up in Sunday school class? Do any of these try to make things you

know aren't okay seem okay? Do any of them try to make you believe that the most important thing is how people look on the outside? Do any of these make fun of a particular group of people or Christian beliefs? Cross off everything on your list that does any of these things—and make your best effort not to watch, listen to, or read those things anymore. They are taking up God-space. Look for songs, reading material, and television programs that allow you to give God more space in your life and support the life you're trying to live for him.

- Make a list of things you'd really like to have right now but don't— things like trendy clothes, jewelry, fun stuff to play with, computer or stereo items, or materials for your hobby. You get the idea. Look at each thing on your list and (you guessed it) think and pray about each one. Do you want this item just because everybody else has it? Is it likely to go out of style within a year? Do you want it because it might get other people's attention? Do you want it just because you're bored with the stuff you already have? Do you believe that *not* having this particular thing will make you feel left out and not as important as everybody else? If you answered yes to any of these questions, cross that item off your list and replace it with something about which you can answer no. It doesn't have to be a physical thing, although it can be. For instance, you might cross off the Back Street Boys CD you want only because all your friends have it and write in that CD of old Broadway show tunes you have always secretly wanted but never admitted to a soul. The truer you are to the person God made you to be, the more he likes it.

- Now, this is the most difficult one. Make a list of anything you do or say when you're with other people just so they will accept you. Those would be things like whispering about other people behind their backs, being loud and rowdy out in public, playing practical jokes, or using ugly language. Then think and pray about each item. Would you feel uncomfortable saying or doing this around your pastor or some other adult you respect? If so, what can you do about it? First, ask for God's help. He is eager to help you get rid of any speech or behaviors that take up your God-space. Second, ask a good friend to help you by letting you know what you are doing—that way you can stop and walk away. Third, tell your mom or some other adult you trust what you are trying to do. Ask that person to pray for you and give you support. Fourth (and this is very important), stop hanging out with the people you do it with, at least for a while. Fill up that time with people who *don't* do that stuff. Fifth, make a little reminder card and keep it in your pocket or your backpack or your desk at school. Every time you see it, whisper a little prayer for God's help.

Talking to God About It

The "trick" to making more space for God isn't just a matter of shoving out the bad stuff; you need to fill up that space with good stuff—God stuff. Rather than bowing down to friends and fads, bow down to God.

Before you start imagining yourself getting on your knees in the school cafeteria and making a spectacle of yourself, know this: there are cool, private ways to worship God at any time and neat ways to put God first so the new clothes and the "in" group don't get in the way.

Try some of these ways to worship God all day long:

- Wear a cross or special bracelet—something that will remind you that God's always there. When you happen to notice it gleaming in the sun or dangling from your arm, quickly and silently say, "Thanks, God. You're the best."
- Always bow your head and say at least a silent prayer before you eat, even in the school cafeteria. You don't have to make a huge deal out of it; just take a few seconds to thank God. If someone makes fun of

you, say a silent prayer for that person. You'll probably find out that most people will respect what you're doing.

- Play a game with yourself whenever you have time on your hands— like when you've finished the geography test before everyone else or you're waiting in line at the water fountain. Look at the people around you and try to see Christ in each one of them. Is it in the way she let somebody go ahead of her in line? Is it in the way he punched his buddy on the arm to show he likes him (who understands boys, you know)? Before you know it, you realize you're surrounded by God!
- Keep tabs of how many times in a day God is good to you. You can make marks on a piece of paper or even put those sticker stars on it. When you do well on your spelling test, avoid getting hit in the head with a softball, get a fun note from your friend, find a book you've been wanting to read in the library, manage *not* to have a fight with your brother or sister, or snuggle up next to your dad on the couch, give God a star or a check mark. He's the one who sent that little piece of joy your way. By the end of the day, you'll be able to see how good God is to you.
- Look for a visible sign of God in nature every single day. Even if you live in the city, you can do this—even cities have sky and clouds and stuff growing up through the cracks in the sidewalks. Each time you notice something, tell God how amazing he is to have created it.
- Sing "God songs" in the shower.
- Speak out loud to God at least once a day, usually when you're alone, although you don't have to be alone.
- Once in a while, when you're by yourself in a quiet place, *do* "bow down" to God. It makes bowing down to anything else seem as completely ridiculous as it is!

If I could take God anyplace I wanted and tell him how amazing I think he is, here's where we'd go and here's what I'd say.

Well, Shut My Mouth!

You shall not misuse the name of the
LORD your God, for the LORD will not hold anyone
guiltless who misuses his name.

Exodus 20:7

You shall not give false testimony against your neighbor.

Exodus 20:16

Well, Shut My Mouth!

When you were a little kid, did you ever go running to your mom whining something like, "Mo-om! He called me a re-tard"?

If you did, your mom probably reminded you of a phrase all moms learned in Mom School: "Sticks and stones can break my bones, but words can never hurt me." Or she gave you some variation on that theme like, "Just ignore him and he'll go away."

Whatever her version, if she said that, she wasn't *exactly* right. Although she was trying to comfort you (one of the best things moms learn in Mom School), she was forgetting what we all know: Words *can* hurt. They can hurt *bad*.

It only makes sense, then, that as much as we hate people who wound us with jabs like, "Hey, Fatty!" and "Where'd you get that outfit, the Salvation Army?" we don't want to be the ones throwing the punches.

The trouble is, we sometimes—oh, let's face it, we *often*—hurt others without even realizing it. But we have to be aware of our actions if we're really going to follow the commandments at the beginning of this chapter to the letter.

HOW IS THIS A God Thing?

Jesus was pretty clear about this whole issue. The Pharisees were giving him a hard time because his disciples didn't wash their hands before they ate, which was supposedly a big God thing, at the time. Jesus got right to the point—right to what's really important. He said,

**"What goes into a man's mouth does not make him 'unclean,'
but what comes out of his mouth, that is what makes him 'unclean.'"**
Matthew 15:11

**"The things that come out of the mouth come from the heart, and
these make a man 'unclean.' For out of the heart come evil thoughts,
murder, adultery, sexual immorality, theft, false testimony, slander."**
Matthew 15:18–19

Basically, Jesus is saying that what you say—what comes out of your mouth—is one of the most important ways to tell if your heart is right. Do you want to be unclean in God's eyes? Then go ahead and say something ugly about that girl you can't stand. Feel free to cuss when everybody else does. Don't give a second thought to making fun of your friends—after all, you're only kidding.

But who wants to be unclean? We're trying to clean up our acts, and a great way to start is by watching what comes out of our hearts, straight through our mouths.

CHECK Yourself OUT

Just in case you're still saying, "But I never use the Lord's name in vain!" or "I wouldn't bear false witness against my neighbor if you tortured me!" let's take a closer look. Being *way* honest with yourself (this may mean completing the quiz in a closet!), put a check next to each of these things that you have *never* done in your *whole* life:

_____ Said a word you wouldn't want your parents to hear you say

_____ Used slang to make fun of somebody, even behind that person's back ("she's stupid," "he's a major loser," etc.)

_____ Replaced a "swear word" with something milder, even though you still meant the same thing

_____ Used your group's private slang to let somebody else know she *wasn't* in your group

_____ Teased somebody, and he or she didn't laugh

_____ Teased somebody, and that person cried

_____ Teased somebody because you wanted that person to cry

_____ Talked back to your mom or dad in a sarcastic tone

_____ Muttered something under your breath after your mom, dad, or teacher said something to you

_____ Said something sarcastic and felt rude afterward

_____ Said something negative, but true, about somebody behind that person's back

_____ Said something negative about somebody behind that person's back that you weren't sure was true

_____ Said something negative about somebody behind that person's back that you knew wasn't true

_____ Exaggerated while telling about something that happened

_____ Exaggerated while telling something about yourself or your family

_____ Stretched the truth a little to keep from getting into trouble

_____ Kept your mouth shut while somebody else told something you knew was a lie

If you didn't put a check mark next to any of the above, please call me and I will nominate you for sainthood! We have all done more than one of these things, so much so that we're not even going to "score" this quiz. Just taking it reminds us that we all have mouths we need to keep a tighter rein on. We can't just say, "Oh, everybody does it—I'm only human." Not if we want to love God with everything we have and love our neighbors as ourselves (remember those two great commandments?).

But how do we control our words? It seems like even though we know it's wrong to lie, exaggerate, gossip, and backstab, our lips just fly open and stuff comes pouring out on its own. What's up with that?

Girlz WANT TO KNOW

✿ *LILY: Sure, I talk about people, but it's because I'm trying to be better or I want them to be better. You know, like I'll tell Reni that Zooey needs to stop thinking she has every disease in the world, stuff like that. That isn't gossiping, is it?*

There's what we call a fine line between out-and-out lying, backstabbing, rumor passing, and gossip, and it usually starts with, "I don't mean to talk about her, but. . . ." We're better off if we pretend that line doesn't exist and just decide never to discuss people's faults with friends. If Zooey really does have a problem with being a hypochondriac, or you think Suzy's shyness is interfering with her grades, or Kresha isn't getting enough attention from her mom, then talk to a grown-up about getting some help. Or talk to *her* and tell her you're her friend and you're worried about her.

✿ *ZOOEY: Sometimes Ashley and Chelsea and people like that make me so mad I want to scream! I know we're not supposed to say ugly stuff about people, but it makes me feel better if I can tell Lily or Suzy how evil Ashley treated me.*

That's called **venting**, and it definitely makes you feel better—but not for long. Have you noticed how, after a little while, the anger just comes flooding back in and you have to vent again? Besides that, I bet you also feel kind of crummy at times after you've raked Ashley and Chelsea over the coals.

There are a couple of things you can do instead of venting. First, vent in a way that doesn't hurt anybody. Write out your anger in your journal. Go to a private place and rant out loud to God about it. Do something physical—run, swim, or punch a pillow—to get that energy out. But don't stop there. The second thing is to work on changing the situation that makes you angry. Can you stop trying to be friends with Ashley and Chelsea and just hang out with people who don't put you down? Can you ask your teacher to move you so you don't have to sit near them in class? Can you tell *them* how upset you get when they're mean to you? It's been said that craziness is doing something the same way every time and expecting different results. Don't be crazy!

✿ *SUZY: I say words like "gosh" and "darn," and a lady at my church told me I shouldn't even say those because they're just substitutes for the words I'm not saying. But if I don't mean it that way, does that make it swearing?*

That's a toughie. Jesus does say that we shouldn't use "expletives" at all, just say yes or no and let it go at that (Matthew 5:33–37, if you want to read it). But, yikes, when you're ticked off or excited, it seems like you have to say *some-thing*! Maybe you can think of it this way. You haven't been swearing if you didn't realize phrases like "Oh, my gosh" are substitutes for "Oh, my God." Now that

BUMMER!

Dude!

somebody's brought that to your attention, it's possible that you might offend someone by using those expressions. It isn't the biggest deal in life (some people have way too much time on their hands if they're sitting around thinking about that!), but just to be on the safe side, maybe you can think of other ways to express anger, disappointment, excitement. There's nothing wrong with expressions like: "Oh, rats!" "Bummer." "Aw, man." "Dude!" "Yikes!" "Wow!" "Cool!" "Oops!" You can even try some vari-

Cool!

ations on those like: "Yikester!" "Dude-let!" "Ratskies!" Just remember that your language ought to lift people up rather than tear them down. Do

Yikester!

what you can, and if you make an unconscious mistake, ask God to forgive you and move on. Determine to do better. One little gosh never kept anybody out of heaven!

✿ **_RENI: If we're not supposed to talk about people, then what's left to talk about? I think us Girlz would end up just sitting around looking at each other!_**

Most of us, even adults, wind up discussing who said what and who did what and to whom because it's easier than talking about almost anything else. But with a little effort, we really _can_ think of more interesting things to jack our jaws about. What about events, experiences, things that have happened? Wouldn't you rather hear about what it was like for Kresha growing up in Croatia than that she thinks Ashley Adamson is a snob? Wouldn't it be more interesting to know what Suzy does in soccer camp than what Shad Shifferdecker said to her in the lunch line?

You're also getting to the age where you can talk about ideas as well as people, places, and things (those other nouns!). Wouldn't it be fun to discuss what the future's going to be like? How much your interests have changed since last year? Whether the dress code is fair? What kind of music you like and why? It takes a little more effort than just looking across the cafeteria and saying, "Look at that girl's outfit. Is that ugly or what?" But anything *really* worth doing is going to take some effort. Make it a game among your friends: What can we talk about that doesn't put other people down? Trust me, you won't let yourselves sit in silence for long!

Just Do It

It isn't easy to change when it comes to our talking habits. In fact, it's probably simpler to stop biting your nails or give up Snickers bars than it is to break the habit of gossiping, white-lying, exaggerating, sarcasm, and hurtful teasing. The problem is, we don't always realize we're doing these things or how much they hurt other people.

The best way to start changing is to follow these steps:

1. Take one thing at a time, like gossiping or being sarcastic to your sister.
2. Plan and take some specific action against it.
3. Replace it with something else.
4. Pray every day for help.

Let's take a look at an example.

Lily looks at the list under Check Yourself Out and decides she really needs to work on not using a sarcastic tone with her mom—things like "Oh, right, Mom, like I'm really going to forget to make my bed when you remind me every single hour." She prays about it and talks to her youth pastor some and decides she should ask her mom to tell her every time she uses a sarcastic tone. Not yell at her, punish her, or tell her she's the worst daughter on the planet—just remind her with something like, "Tone, Lily." Lily vows she'll apologize on the spot and replace her sarcasm with something more respectful, like, "Okay, Mom, I'll make my bed. Thanks for reminding me." Lily knows it isn't going to be easy because she's pretty good at sarcasm, and a lot of people think it's really funny (though not her mother!). She knows she's going to have to do some big-time praying—she can't do this without God.

Now it's your turn.

- Pick something from the Check Yourself Out list that you checked off and that you'd like to work on:

  _____

- Pray about it, asking God to help you find a way to exchange that for something better.
- Come up with a plan of action. Ask for help—from a parent, some other adult you trust, or a friend who seems to have conquered this particular evil. Find some simple way to be reminded "you're doing it again" and come up with a small thing you have to do when it's called to your attention. Maybe your friend gives you a poke in the side, and you have to apologize or change the subject or find another word to use.
- Your plan:

  _____

- Find something to replace that bad habit. Maybe every night during your quiet time you could write down five nice things you can say about that girl you're always bad-mouthing. Perhaps you could come up with a whole new vocabulary list to replace those ugly phrases you tend to toss around. Remember that if you just leave a big empty space where the bad habit used to be, it will probably come back and take up residence again. You have to fill it with a God thing so the bad habit has no hope of squeezing into its old place.
- Your replacement: _____
- Pray. There's no way you can do it alone.

Talking to God About It

Dear _____ *(your favorite way of addressing our Lord),*

I have a real problem with my mouth, which is _____
_____.

Just recently I did it. I _____
_____.

I feel so lousy about that. Will you please forgive me? Will you please

help me to follow a plan for changing that about myself? Will you help me when it gets hard, especially when _____
_____?

I could sure use your help in replacing that with _____
_____.

I know I can't do this without you—and I know you'll be there. You're the best. I love you.

My favorite positive, uplifting, feel-good word is . . .

But Church Is Boring!

Remember the Sabbath day by keeping it holy.
Exodus 20:8

But Church Is Boring!

So what's the big deal about the Sabbath Day anyway? Let's find out. Have any of these thoughts ever gone through your head?

✿ *LILY: "Our Sunday school class is so dumb. All we do is word searches from Bible stories. I beg my parents not to make me go."*

✿ *RENI: "The sermon is so long at our church, I feel like screaming."*

✿ *Suzy: "I know you're not supposed to work on Sundays, but I always have so much homework to do."*

✿ *KRESHA: "If I'm out having fun with my friends on Sunday instead of going to church, isn't that just as holy?"*

✿ *ZOOEY: "My mom won't let me go to church. She says they just want our money. Can I still keep the Sabbath Day holy?"*

Just like a lot of the other commandments, this one sounds easy, but when you get right down to it, it can sometimes be tough. But just like the others, God didn't just hand down the order and then expect us to figure out how to carry it out. He gives us all the instructions.

HOW IS THIS A God Thing?

The descendants of Moses really took the Sabbath commandment seriously and wouldn't even let people lean over and pick something up off the ground on the Sabbath because that would be "working." So when Jesus' hungry disciples went through a grain field and picked themselves something to eat on the Sabbath, the Pharisees flipped out. "Your disciples are doing what is unlawful on the Sabbath!" (Matthew 12:1–2).

Jesus set them straight right away. He told them that God is more important than some picky rule. And then he *really* did some work and healed somebody, right in the synagogue (Matthew 12:3–13).

What that means to us is that, of course, we need to try to set aside Sunday as a day to rest, regroup, give thanks for the past week, and get ready for the next one. But we don't have to be freaked out about it if there's a little homework left to be done or we have to make ourselves a sandwich. Think about it: we'd be in a world of hurt if every doctor said he wouldn't work on Sunday, and you broke your arm or had an attack of appendicitis!

But you will notice that every Sabbath, Jesus was in the synagogue, teaching and worshiping with the others. Part of "keeping it holy" is setting aside time that's just for God, a time where you're taught and can share what you're learning with other seekers.

So the Bible is telling us three things about this fourth commandment:

1. It should mostly be a day to rest.
2. Going to church should be part of our rest.
3. If it's absolutely necessary to do some kind of work, that's okay.

CHECK Yourself OUT

Put a check mark next to the paragraph that best describes your typical Sunday.

_____ I go to Sunday school and church. Then mostly I kick around all afternoon—maybe our family does something or we all just relax. Sunday night we usually go back to church. Sundays are special.

_____ I sometimes go to church on Sunday morning. Then I either have chores to do or my family does something. I usually spend the evening doing homework. Except for going to church, Sundays are pretty much like Saturdays.

_____ I hardly ever go to church on Sundays. Mostly my family does something fun or I just mess around. Sometimes I do chores or homework. Except for not going to school, Sunday seems just about like any other day.

Just Do It

If you checked the first statement, the Sabbath's pretty holy at your house. It's easier for you because your whole family is involved. If you want to make the Sabbath even more holy, try some of these activities:

- Schedule a little quiet time by yourself on Sundays to thank God for the week past and pray about the week to come. Maybe you have a special Sunday spot where you go to pray or a separate Sunday journal or section in your journal.
- Write a note or make a card for someone you really like, telling that person what you like about them and how you thank God they're in your life.
- Treat yourself to something you don't have time for the rest of the week, or set aside something special just for this day. Maybe you would like to reread a book you love or savor that Milky Way bar you've been saving since Wednesday. It could be that you catch up on your scrapbook, press flowers in a book, or learn origami.
- Get as comfortable as you can and listen to music you love. A bathtub full of bubbles is a great place for this.

If you checked the second statement, you're probably going through the motions, but the day doesn't seem terribly special to you. Pray that it will become more holy for you. Try to get your homework and chores done on Saturday. Ask your parents if you can go back to church on Sunday night if there's a good youth program or kids' church going on then. If you want, you can do one or two of the activities listed above. You'll be amazed at how much better your week goes if you do.

If you checked the third statement, you're in a good spot, because no matter what you add, it's going to improve your Sundays! If you don't go to church because your parents don't, ask around among your friends. Find out who goes to a church she really likes, and see if you can go with her. If you don't go to church with your parents because you just don't want to, tag along with them this Sunday or ask if you can go to a friend's church you like more. Then ask God to help you make the whole day more holy. Try to get your homework and chores done on Saturday. Ask if family activities can start after you get home from church, or plan to go at night. If you want, you can even do one or two of the activities listed above. After a while, the holiness you feel will come in the form of smoother weeks with less stress.

Girlz WANT TO KNOW

✿ *LILY: I go to Sunday school, but it's not all that holy. We read a Bible story and do a word search (lame), and then the girls talk to each other and the boys see how many markers they can stick together in one big stick. It's just dumb!*

That is a definite bummer, and it's unfortunately pretty common. First let me give you a pat on the back for caring what your Sunday school class is like and obviously wanting to get more out of it. Then let me suggest a couple of things:

1. Talk to your Sunday school teacher and let him or her know that you aren't learning as much as you'd like. Maybe you even have some suggestions. How about role plays? Or putting on a puppet show for the younger kids? Or a serious discussion about, say, whether those Bible stories are just stories or do they teach us lessons about how to live our lives? If you don't get a response from your teacher, you may want to talk to the head of the whole Sunday school or your pastor. Better yet, ask your mom or dad to speak to someone about it.
2. Don't give up on the whole day just because your class is lame. Participate in the worship service, do some holy activities on your own, and pray that Sunday school will improve.

✿ *KRESHA: Sometimes when we don't go to church on Sunday and I'm with my whole big family—aunts and uncles and cousins and every-*

one—and we're having a picnic, I feel so full of love and I think of God.
Isn't that as good as going to church?

Once in a while, Kresha, I think it is. But if you did that every Sunday, a couple of things would happen:

1. You would miss out on the teaching that church provides. If we're going to become better Christians, constantly growing closer to God, we must keep learning, and the best place to do that is in church and Sunday school. Being with your family is a good place to see evidence of what you've learned, but don't stop learning.
2. You would miss opportunities to serve your fellow Christians. Part of the reason for going to church is so that there will be a "family" of believers. When people in your church family have problems, you're there to help them. When they have sorrows, you're there to cry with them. When they have victories, you're there to celebrate with them. Your own family is very important, but your church family is important too. You need to spend time with them.
3. You would miss out on the mysterious thing that happens when believers sing together and pray together. You get a real sense of God *being* there. That happens more when we're worshiping with others than at any other time. Don't miss it!

✿ *ZOOEY: My mom says churches are all about getting your money and controlling you, and she won't let me go, even with my friends.*

It sounds like your mom has had a bad experience with a church. It's sad that once in a while a church will get its focus wrong and start concentrating on what money can buy or on trying to get everybody to think and talk and act exactly the same way. The good news is that doesn't happen very often. Most churches really just want to help people live the most God-filled lives they can. Yes, they have to have money to run the whole operation, but usually they're more about people than about dollars. Still, how can you convince Mom? Try some of these things:

1. Show your mom this book, especially this chapter. Maybe you could read it out loud to her while she's folding the laundry (or fold the laundry *for* her while *she* reads!).
2. Ask the mom of a friend whose church you like to talk to your mother, perhaps with a promise that if you go to church with them, no one will come knocking at the door asking for money.
3. Ask your mom if she would take you just one time. Let her know that if she feels uncomfortable or her fears are confirmed, you won't ask her to take you again. (Then you need to pray that other opportunities will come up!)

And through it all, Zooey, keep praying. God wants you to have a church family, that's for sure. Ask, and you will receive. Maybe not next Sunday. Maybe not this year. But eventually—and, in the meantime, remember that there are plenty of things you can do on your own to keep the Sabbath holy.

Talking to God About It

Dear _____ *(your favorite name for our Lord),*
I'm jazzed about keeping one whole day sacred just for you—but then, life happens. Could you please help me with these things?
_____ *Getting to church*
_____ *Getting the most I can out of church*
_____ *Having a real church family*
_____ *Getting my homework and chores done before Sunday so I can rest*

_____ *Doing special, holy things on Sundays*

If anybody in my church needs help making the worship experience and Sunday school better, could you please be in their minds and hearts and give them ideas? I especially want _____.

If my parents need help seeing why I want to be part of a church, would you please help them, especially when it comes to _____.

Please, God, help me to make Sunday a day of rest, just like you gave yourself, so that all the rest of my days can be lived for you too.

I love you.

A perfect Sunday for me would be . . .

But Mo-om!

**Honor your father and your mother,
so that you may live long in the land the
LORD your God is giving you.**
Exodus 20:12

But Mo-om!

In *The Buddy Book* (Oh, you haven't read it? Get yourself a copy, girl!), we talked about getting along with your mom and dad. If you follow those guidelines, you should be able to raise a set of pretty happy parents.

Except—sigh—there are always exceptions. Once again, Moses didn't spell those out. Do any of these daughter-thoughts sound familiar?

- I used to think Mom was perfect, but now she messes up all the time. What happened?
- I wish my parents wouldn't hang around us when my friends come over. It's so embarrassing.
- Why does my mom have to pick up every new word I use? I hate it when she tries to act like she's in middle school!
- Mom and Dad still treat me like I'm this baby. You'd think I didn't even have a brain of my own—except I'm supposed to make straight A's with it.
- Just because I'm the oldest (youngest, middle kid, only child), I get treated so unfairly.
- There's no such thing as arguing in our house. They're right, I'm wrong, and I never get to express my opinion.

Yes, you absolutely know you have to honor your mother and father. You wouldn't scream at them, call them names, out-and-out disobey everything they said, or wish they were dead any more than you'd jump off a bridge! But what about the times when you *know* you're right and they're, well, possibly wrong? How do you honor them then?

First, let's see where you are when it comes to those "exceptions." After all, not everybody is feeling those little parent itchies, and that's normal too. Just check out what's going on with you and your mom and dad.

If you've had one of the experiences described below or something similar to it, put a check next to it.

Part I

____ One of your parents made a mistake with you, and even though he or she admitted it, you didn't get an apology.

____ Your mom or dad yelled at you in front of your friends.

____ Your mom or dad told an embarrassing story about you in front of people who are important to you.

____ Your parents have talked about you to people as if you weren't even in the room.

____ Your mom or dad read your private diary or journal.

____ You were punished for something you didn't do.

____ One of your parents believed a lie your brother or sister told about you.

Part II

____ Your parents won't let you go to church or attend church activities.

____ Your parents aren't Christians and you are, or would like to be, or at least would like to know more about it.

____ Your parents are divorced and that makes you unhappy.

____ Your parents have fights that upset you.

____ You hardly ever see your parents.

Part III

____ One of your parents is abusive.

____ The drinking habit of one of your parents is affecting the family.

____ Your parents aren't making sure that you have enough food and clothes and medical care. You miss meals and are left at home a lot without adult supervision.

If you had check marks *only* in Part I, the kinds of mistakes you think your parents are making are the ones all parents make from time to time. They're doing their best. They sometimes run into situations that just aren't as easy to handle as they look. Imagine you're a parent. How do you know which of your kids is telling the truth? How do you always know what's going to be embarrassing to your daughter when she's changing so fast? It used to be okay to look at the stuff in her room. When did that change? See how tough it is?

The best way to handle Part I situations is to talk to your parents about them—when you *aren't* ready to pitch a fit, when you can be calm and simply state your case. Try something like this: "Mom, if I mess up when my friends are here, could you take me aside instead of yelling at me in front of them?"

That's not to say that you will always get your way or that your parents will like being told that you don't like what they're doing. But try, and pray about it too. It is so much better than flouncing to your room and slamming the door, yelling back at your parents, or getting on the phone and venting to your friends. None of those things will solve the problem. Talking it out just might. That's honoring your parents.

If you had *any* checks in Part II, you really need to talk with a wise and trusted adult. These issues are too difficult to handle alone—you'll want someone who is willing to listen to you, pray with or for you, perhaps talk to your parents and get their perspective, and/or suggest some possible solutions.

If you're concerned about church-related things, like your parents don't go to church with you or they don't want you to go at all, talk to a friend's pastor or youth minister. If you're having trouble with the way your parents get along, talk to your school counselor or a friend's mom or dad you can trust. Other adult relatives can sometimes be helpful too. Of course, the best thing is to go to your parents if you feel safe doing that. They may not even realize how their relationship is affecting you. Parents, no matter what they're going through, love their kids. They want you to be happy, but they may just be wrapped up in their own problems. Remind them that you need their help. That's honoring your mother and father.

If you had *any* checks in Part III, be very sure you're being honest with yourself. Do you *really* miss meals, or are you just sick of McDonald's because your parents are too busy to cook? Do one or both of your parents really abuse you, or do you just resent it because they raise their voices? Is drinking really a problem for one of your parents, or do you just feel that one glass of wine a week is a sin? If you know in your heart that any of the things listed in Part III is truly going on in your house, go *immediately* to an adult you trust and tell that person the truth. It's scary, but it's the right thing to do. Moms and dads who are abusing alcohol, abusing each other or their children, or neglecting their family's basic needs need help as much as you do. Telling someone who can help is honoring your mother and father.

Girlz WANT TO KNOW

Sometimes the my-mom-is-wrong issues kind of fall between the cracks of the categories, and there's no clear-cut way to deal with them. Let's look at a few of those situations.

✿ *LILY: My dad is, like, super intelligent, and sometimes when my friends are over, he tells jokes nobody gets. Don't get me wrong—I really love my dad—but I wish he could be as cool and funny as, like, Reni's dad.*

So your dad's a geek, huh, Lily? That may be true by the standards of your age group. But think about it: do you really want your dad to act like he's nineteen—especially when you need his advice, his wisdom, his experience, his hug before you go to bed at night? The thing is, you can't really expect your dad to tell jokes like a twenty-year-old comedian when your friends are over, be all wise and sage when you've got a problem, *and* Mr. Intelligence when you desperately need help with your homework. Take Dad as he is—that's honoring him. Oh, and ask Reni. I bet *she* doesn't think her dad is always "cool."

✿ *ZOOEY: My mom treats me so different from my brother. He—*

Oops, stop right there, Zooey. There's a really good reason why you're treated differently than your brother. You *are* different from him! He's not only a different gender and a different age and at a different place in the family, but he has a totally different personality from yours. He has different needs, wants, interests, moods, quirks, strengths, and weaknesses. While you should both be treated the same in some areas, such as the amount of love you receive, the quality of medical care you receive, and the level of nutrition you're provided, there is no way you can both be dealt with in exactly identical ways when it comes to things like school expectations, punishments, the amount of individual time your mom spends with you each day, even household chores.

Dealing with this issue is actually good practice for adult life because, like it or not, the world isn't going to treat you fairly. We all have to find ways to be happy even when things don't come out even. Try keeping a list of all the good things about the way your mom treats you—maybe she loves to go shopping with you, or she never makes you take out the garbage or mow the lawn, or she still cuddles you when you need it. You'll see just how good she really is to you. Don't bother comparing anything with the way she handles your brother. It isn't worth your time.

✿ *KRESHA: My mom came to a meeting at my school with my teachers wearing an outfit a teenager would wear. I was so embarrassed that I wanted to throw my coat over her! How can I make sure she doesn't do that again?*

Whether you should do anything at all depends on why she wore the outfit. If she liked it and had fun wearing it and felt good in it (and it wasn't something immodest, which I doubt), then, you go, Mom! There's not a thing wrong with that. Where are the rules that say what a "Mom" is supposed to look like, anyway? I bet half your friends who saw her were thinking, "I wish my mom dressed that cool."

On the other hand, if you know your mom is dressing young because she's feeling old or she's trying to be more like you or she wants you to think she's hip, that's another thing. It still doesn't mean she should be locked in the closet until she gets some taste, but you can help her feel better about herself simply by telling her how much you appreciate it that she can always give you good advice, that she has her feet on the ground, unlike your friends who are as confused as you are! Compliment her when she dresses in a more mature fashion. Tell her you think she's great just the way she is. Just don't ever mention the young outfits themselves. If you've soothed her fears, she may stop wearing them. If not, how is it really hurting you? Half the things we get embarrassed about aren't even noticed by others!

Just Do It

Ready to try to deal with one of your parent problems yourself? Here we go.

Step 1

Think back over the last week and see if you can come up with the last thing one of your parents did that you thought was wrong. Don't just choose something that made you unhappy, like "I got grounded for smacking my brother." Pick an incident where it seemed to you that one of your parents made a mistake: _____

Lily's problem: I was talking to my dad about a problem I had. I went through the whole thing and asked him what I should do. He just looked at me and said, "What, Lilliputian? I must have gotten distracted." Why won't he ever listen to me?

Step 2

Talk to God about it. The solution to any problem starts with prayers. Lily's prayer:

God, could you please help me? I'm so tired of my dad not hearing what I'm saying because he's so wrapped up in his work and stuff.

*I really need your help with a solution, especially if there's something
I need to be doing.*

Step 3

Imagine that incident going the way *you* would have liked. Think
it through thoroughly. It might help to write it down or even draw it in a series
of pictures, like a comic strip.

Lily's imagined scene: I walk into Dad's study, and he immediately puts
his pen down and closes his book. He folds his hands on the desk, leans across
it, and says, "What's wrong, Lilliputian? You look upset." I tell him the whole
story and he nods the whole time, and when I'm done, he comes out from
behind the desk and sits next to me and helps me figure out what to do. The
phone rings once while we're talking, but he lets the answering machine get it.

Step 4

Look at your imagined scene and think about your parent. Are
there parts of it that your mom or dad are just never going to do in a
thousand years because it just isn't him or her? Cross out those parts. After
all, we can't expect our parents to have personality transplants just to make
life easier for us!

What Lily crossed out: No matter what, her dad is into his work. Even if
the living room suddenly blew up, he wouldn't put his pen down *immediately*.
He'd have to finish that sentence. She also crossed out *"What's wrong,
Lilliputian? You look upset."* Once she told him she was upset, he'd be concerned—but he isn't going to figure that out himself unless Lily is hysterical,
and she knows that. *"He comes out from behind the desk."* Nah. He really
likes it back there, and what does it matter, anyway?

Step 5

Go to Mom or Dad with what you have left and simply say, "I
sure wish it could go this way." That is, if you still need to. Maybe

you've figured out by now that you're expecting an awful lot—that it isn't going to change, and maybe it's you who needs to change to adjust to it. If that's the case, go on to Step 6.

What Lily says to Dad: "Dad, I wish when I had a problem you could stop what you're doing and thinking about and listen to me. You know, close your book so you won't get distracted by it. I'd love that."

Step 6

Think about *your* part in changing the scene. After all, if you're expecting your parents to treat you as if you're older, you have to act older. Take some of the responsibility sometimes instead of always requiring them to do everything right. Wouldn't you hate to have to know what every person in the house needed, wanted, thought, and felt every minute of the day? Practice your part for the next time a situation comes up. Write it down so you won't forget your plan.

Lily's plan for next time: Ask Dad when would be a good time to talk about my problem, a time when he isn't going to be busy. Then when we sit down together, ask him if he would mind closing his book so he doesn't get distracted, since that happens a lot. If that doesn't work, go to Mom with my problems. She can do eighty-seven things at the same time and keep track of them all.

I am going to be the perfect mother.

_____
_____
_____
_____
_____
_____
_____
_____
_____
_____
_____
_____
_____
_____

I Can't Help It— I Hate Her!

You shall not murder.
Exodus 20:13

I Can't Help It—I Hate Her!

You can feel your face turning red. You're gritting your teeth like you're trying to crack a walnut between them. The hair on the back of your neck is standing up. Your eyes have gone into slits. Why?

Because *she*—or *he*—is passing by you. She hasn't said anything—yet—but she will. You can count on it. And then it will be all you can do not to rip off the wallpaper. You know it's just plain wrong to hate another human being, but she—ooh—she makes you so hateful!

We've all come across that person in our lives, the one who brings out the worst in us. It could be the teacher who yells at you for everything. Maybe it's that boy who always makes fun of you. Perhaps it's some girl who cuts you down every time you walk by.

It doesn't have to be someone you despise *all* the time. There's a good chance you only "hate" your brother when he's teasing you about your chubby cheeks in front of some boy you like. You probably "hate" your soft-ball coach only when he reams you for striking out.

Whatever the situation, most of us have been guilty of full-blown hate. And even though we haven't planned murders or other kinds of evil revenge, we've felt the beginnings of the same kind of anger that drives people to hurt the people they hate. We better learn how to nip this one in the bud, and fast!

HOW IS THIS A God Thing?

Jesus knew his people really well. He knew what they needed to hear: that just because you don't commit actual murder doesn't mean you haven't broken commandment number six.

Here's what he told the folks he taught: "You have heard that it was said to the people long ago, 'Do not murder, and anyone who murders will be subject to judgment.' . . . But anyone who says, 'You fool!' will be in danger of the fire of hell" (Matthew 5:21–22).

Do you get what that means? It's tight—it's asking a *lot*. Jesus is saying, don't let yourself get angry enough to even *think* about calling a person a name. That's right up there with breaking out your AK–47.

Before you get all depressed and decide you can't live up to that, read on. Jesus tells us what to do *instead*. (Isn't that just like him?)

He says the minute you realize you've got something against someone— or that person has something against you—drop everything and go work it out (Matthew 5:23–25). And don't wait for somebody else to settle it. Don't let it go that far. Deal with stuff before you start committing murder in your heart.

CHECK Yourself OUT

It's always easy to read about those "morons" in the Bible and think, "I wouldn't have acted like that. If I'd been there, I'd have known *exactly* what Jesus was talking about."

Really? Let's see.

Read each statement and choose the ending that fits you best. Be really honest. After all, the only way to solve a problem is to first admit you have one.

1.   Of all the people I know right now,

_____ a. there are a lot of people who can't stand me.

_____ b. there are some people who don't like me.

_____ c. everybody loves me—or at least likes me.

2.   When it comes to enemies, I

_____ a. have several.

_____ b. have maybe one or two.

_____ c. don't have any.

3.   I get angry at a certain person

_____ a. every time I even think about him or her.

_____ b. almost every time I see him or her.

_____ c. now and then, if I have to be around him or her for a while.

4.   If I were invited to a cool party, but a person I disliked was going to be there too, I would

_____ a. definitely not go.

_____ b. go but be sure not to speak to or be close to that person.

_____ c. go and not even think about that person.

5. If a person I have a problem with gives me a bad time, I

_____ a. lash out somehow, even if it's just with words.

_____ b. walk away before I lash out, but I sure *want* to smack or yell or something!

_____ c. don't really feel like doing anything to the person.

This is a very short quiz because most of us don't like to think about hate for too long. Hopefully, this is enough to help you see where you stand on the subject—and it may be on a spot you hadn't suspected.

Count your a's, b's and c's and write the totals in the spaces provided:

_____a's

_____b's

_____c's

If you had more a's than other letters, hatred and its "mother," anger, have a pretty tight hold on you. That doesn't make you a murderer! It just makes you a person with some work to do with God. Read on and, in the meantime, stay away from that person or people you dislike until we get a handle on this thing.

If you had more b's than other letters, you're controlling hatred and its "mom," anger, but it's still there, clouding your thoughts and keeping you from being as happy as you could be. You and God together can work on it. Read on. Remember that just because you can control hate and anger most of the time, that doesn't mean they aren't still bad for you.

If you had more c's than other letters, hatred and anger aren't things you feel often. That could be because you're really at peace with yourself and your world, which is great. Or it could be because you think being angry with another person is totally wrong, so you bury it inside you somewhere. Or it could be because you just haven't come across a person who pushes your hate button yet. Just in case, read on. It never hurts to know how to handle the very human emotion of anger when it flares up.

When we read the Gospels, we don't hear Jesus teaching people how to take out their anger on a punching bag or run five miles to get rid of hateful feelings. He tells them—and us—to turn our anger and its "child" hatred into something else. That something, if you'll recall, is love.

Jesus says, "You have heard that it was said, 'Love your neighbor and hate your enemy.' But I tell you: Love your enemies and pray for those who persecute you. . . . If you love [only] those who love you, what reward will you get?" (Matthew 5:43–44, 46).

Right. That oughta be about as easy as driving a Buick up somebody's nose. How are we supposed to *love* our enemies?

Girlz WANT TO KNOW

❁ *LILY: Okay—Shad Shifferdecker—hello! I can't even force myself to like him, much less love him!*

Who said you had to like him? Liking has nothing to do with it. Let's look at what Jesus means by love. He says pray for those who persecute you (Matthew 5:44). He tells us not to hurt them. In fact, he tells us to turn the other cheek when they hurt us (Matthew 5:39). You don't have to find Shad Shifferdecker's finer qualities and start hanging out with him and become best friends. You may *never* like him. But you can pray for him (heaven knows, there's plenty of material there!). You can hope for the best for him instead of relishing the thought of him walking off a cliff. You can just turn away when he starts in on you and take away his opportunity for being hateful to you. That's loving him. But *like* him—nah!

❁ *RENI: That whole forgiveness thing—I don't get that. When Shad left me lying on the ground unconscious in the middle of the night, I was supposed to say, "Oh, that's okay, Shad. No big deal"?*

No way! Forgiveness doesn't mean you tell the person what he did wasn't wrong. The whole point is that it *was* wrong, but you aren't going to hold it against him for the rest of your life. What Shad did was horrible, and he ought to know how terrible it was for you. If he doesn't, you should tell him. You might never trust him again. You probably won't become his best bud. But you aren't going to walk around with a big hard place in your heart with his name on it either. That would just keep you from ever trusting *anybody* or becoming anybody else's best bud. Forgiveness means letting it go, not holding a grudge, not letting it make you hateful. It doesn't mean letting him off the hook. He still has to take responsibility for his actions.

❁ *ZOOEY: Even though Ashley and her friends are really mean to me, I keep loving them and forgiving them. But it doesn't seem to make any difference—they still treat me like I'm a pot of dirt. What am I doing wrong?*

You're doing some things very right, actually. God's proud of you, I'm sure, for loving and forgiving. However, God didn't promise that your actions would change the other person. He only promised that it would change *you.* You have become kind, loving, forgiving, and generous. They have not. So why would you want to be around them? Why continue to let yourself be beat up by girls who don't know a thing about loving and forgiving and kindness? Don't give them a chance to be mean to you. Steer clear of them. Hang with the Girlz, who truly love you and would never treat you that way. Ashley and Chelsea's meanness to you has nothing to do with who you are—it has to do with who *they* are. Keep praying for them, but stay away from them.

✿ *SUZY: I have an uncle who drinks too much and yells too much and is always making my aunt and my cousins cry. I just can't stop hating him. Sometimes I even wish he would drink enough to put him in a coma he would never come out of. What can I do to get all this hate out of me?*

You're right to want it out of you. That kind of thing just eats away at you. But you're also right that it's very hard not to hate someone when you see him hurting the people you love. It's so hard that there's no way you can do this alone. You need God's help—your whole family does. If your parents are Christians, or at least open to it, ask them to pray with you, not only that your heart will be softened but that your uncle's will too.

Get as many people as you can to pray about the situation. Knowing God is at work to change things will help you. Focus on love instead of hate. Shower your cousins with love. Send them letters and tapes of neat music and little presents. Talk to them whenever you can, just to let them know you care, that you think they're special, that you're always around for them. Hate can't grow when love is taking up all the room.

Just Do It

Thinking about all the things you've read in this chapter, maybe you have some ideas about a person who sets your teeth on edge and how you can turn your hate into the kind of love Jesus was talking about. Here's a fun way to put that to work.

Notice the four cartoon boxes on the next page.

- In Box One, draw a picture of this person doing some hateful thing he or she has done in the past.
- In Box Two, draw a picture of you "hating" this person. Make yourself look as hateful as you imagine you did when this nasty thing happened.

- In Box Three, draw a picture of you doing something loving about the situation. Are you comforting somebody who was hurt by the person? Are you praying for that hateful person? Would you consider writing a letter to that person, offering your forgiveness and asking to be left alone? Before you draw the next box, *do* the thing you drew in box three, if that's possible. Notice how you feel now. You might even look in the mirror.
- In Box Four, draw a picture of you now. Compare it to Box Two. Need I say more?

Talking to God About It

Dear _____ *(your favorite way of addressing our Lord)*,

I have a big problem with this person I—I don't like to use this word in your presence, but I have to be honest—this person I hate: _____.

I'm sorry for having these feelings. What happens to me when I feel like this is _____. Please forgive me. Please heal these feelings in me.

God, could you please help me find a way to love _____? Please help me to

_____ forgive him/her.

_____ pray for him/her.

_____ hope for the best for him/her.

_____ stop wishing him/her harm.

_____ get myself out of the way so he/she can't hurt me anymore.

I also want to replace my hatred with love, God. Can you help me to find a way and then have the courage to do it? I'm really struggling with the idea of _____.

I want to love the way you love, but there's no way I can do it alone. Please soften my heart and help me to love instead of hate. I know one thing for sure—I love you.

If I had to come up with five good things to say about a person I really dislike, they would be . . .

Shouldn't I Have That?

You shall not steal.
Exodus 20:15

**You shall not covet ... anything that
belongs to your neighbor.**
Exodus 20:17

Shouldn't I Have That?

Okay, so when you're two years old, you walk into somebody else's playroom and you figure everything in there is fair game.

"Mine!" you yell when the owner of that Barbie doll tries to take it away from you. Then when some adult comes in and gives Barbie back to her rightful owner, you throw yourself down on the floor and scream.

But that's when you were two. Things change radically when you get older—at least on the outside.

For one thing, you don't walk into your best friend's room now and say, "I like that poster. I'm taking that home with me." And when your friend says, "Uh, no. You can't have it," you don't hurl yourself down on her bed and kick and scream until her mom comes in and—

I mean—honestly—you can't even *imagine* it!

But what's going on *inside* when you see something somebody else has and you want that thing for yourself? You may not *say*, "I want that. Give it to me." But doesn't the thought, or something like it, sometimes flip through your mind?

I wish I had one of those. How come she always gets the good stuff and I don't? I deserve to have one!

You may be thinking, *Well, sure, but I don't say stuff like that, so isn't that okay?*

Is it? And is it okay to glance at the test answer sheet when the teacher leaves it lying out on her desk in plain sight? Or to keep a twenty-dollar bill you find in the hallway without trying to find out who dropped it? Or to point out that the girl who beat you in the spelling contest can't do math worth a flip?

We're getting into some tough stuff here. We'd better hurry up and get to the bottom line on this, huh?

HOW IS THIS A God Thing?

As usual, Jesus gets right down to the nitty-gritty when it comes to stuff like this. He doesn't just remind us not to want something somebody else has and certainly not to steal it. He says to change the way we think about that "something."

For instance, if you are dying of envy because your friend just got a pair of Capri pants and you don't yet have a pair, Jesus is saying, directly to you: "And why do you worry about clothes? See how the lilies of the field grow. They do not labor or spin. Yet I tell you that not even Solomon in all his splendor was dressed like one of these. If that is how God clothes the grass of the field, which is here today and tomorrow is thrown into the fire, will he not much more clothe you?" (Matthew 6:28–30).

He's not saying don't think about Capri pants. He's saying don't worry about not having them. God loves you so much, he's going to make sure you have what you really need, and it will be much better than what you *think* you need.

According to Jesus, it's okay to save up for a pair of Capri pants, ask your mom to buy you some, or put them on your birthday list for Grandma. But he's also saying it's not okay to stress yourself out about them or wish your friend would gain ten pounds and give them to you!

✓ CHECK Yourself OUT

We know by now that we *all* fall short in a lot of areas. Let's look at this quiz as one more chance to find out what you and God need to work on together.

Imagine that you're trying out for the leading role in a play. It's way important to you, but there's another girl who's *really* good. She and one other girl are your biggest competition. The day of the tryouts, you see one of the girls put a rock where the other will trip on it on the playground. The girl sprains her ankle and doesn't do as well in the tryouts as she might have. You get the part. Would you—

    a. go to the teacher and tell her what you saw, even if that means you don't get the part after all.

    b. tell your friends that you feel bad about what happened and ask them not to tell as you go on with rehearsals.

    c. keep the whole thing to yourself because you're afraid you might lose that part you wanted so much.

Have you been really honest with yourself? What action would you *really* choose? Be sure it isn't just the answer you think you *should* choose. Hard, isn't it?

If you chose a, it means you're following God's commandment to the letter, even though it might not work out the best for you. I don't know about you, but I hope that's what I'd do.

If you chose b, it shows some good on your part. After all, you might be thinking, you do feel bad for the girl who was hurt. And it wasn't you who tripped her up, for Pete's sake. But ask yourself this—if you hadn't been in the tryouts, or if you hadn't gotten the part, would you have said something to the teacher? Choice **a** is still the best one.

If you chose c, you might be thinking, *Come on! Is it really my business to tattle on someone else? I'll do a great job on the role. Maybe this is my big chance to show 'em what I can do. Maybe God wants me to have this—*

Uh . . . no. God never wants us to do anything less than what he commands. He forgives us when we don't quite make it. He understands why we don't. But he still expects us to always try, try, try to do the right thing.

Let's look at how you can do that—how you can come closer to doing the God thing.

Girlz WANT TO KNOW

✿ *LILY: My teacher asked me to get the scissors out of her desk drawer, and when I opened it, I saw the social studies test we were having the next day. There, right where I could see it, was the big essay question. It was no big deal for me because I always study for tests and I don't have any trouble with essays—in fact, I could go on for days! But Zooey has so many problems with them and she's trying so hard to make better grades so she can be with Reni, Suzy, and me in honors classes next year in middle school. At recess, I told Zooey I would tutor her for the test, and when I did I used that real essay question as my example. I helped her write out the whole thing and practically memorize it—but I didn't tell her that was the real question. The next day, she did great on that test, and she was so proud of herself. It's not like I gave her the answers, so I don't think it's really cheating, but how come I feel so guilty?*

You feel guilty, Lily honey, because you *are* guilty. You took advantage of the situation. Bottom line: that's cheating. And when you were coaching Zooey, didn't you suggest some things for her to put in her essay answer? Would she have known what to write if she'd gotten the question cold on the test? Basically, she "cheated" without even knowing it. So what would God have had you do? Perhaps tell your teacher you saw the test and ask her to change the essay question so you wouldn't be tempted to coach Zooey on the right question. Or don't tutor Zooey for the test at all, but ask Reni or Suzy to do it so there's no way you can cheat for Zooey. I know it sounds picky, but God's that way. He loves and forgives us no matter what we do, but he expects us to try to do our absolute best.

✿ *RENI: We were on our way from the orchestra room to the auditorium to do our first concert for the whole student body, and I realized I didn't have my copy of the first piece we were playing. I couldn't find it in my folder or around my chair, and I was panicking. Everybody got up to go, and I saw that the girl next to me had left hers on her music stand. So I grabbed it and took off. When we got to the stage, I saw her get this scared look on her face and she asked our teacher if she could go back to the room to get something. He said no, that we were starting, and she had to play the first piece from memory. I saw how scared she was that she was going to mess up. I felt bad, but I didn't pass her music to her. What should I have done?*

You should have passed her the music, of course. Every note she missed, every embarrassed second she had during the playing of that piece was pretty much your responsibility. Granted, if you hadn't picked up the music and taken it with you, she wouldn't have been allowed to go back to the room anyway. She did forget it on her own. But what about *your* copy? You'd have been in the same position if you hadn't picked up hers. And yes, now there is only one person messing up instead of two because she doesn't have her music, but the end doesn't make how you got there okay. Tell your friend what happened. Apologize to her. And keep track of your stuff!

✿ *ZOOEY: Sometimes I feel really bad about how jealous I am of Lily and Reni and Suzy. They're all so pretty and smart and talented. I'm not any of those things. I'm chubby and I have trouble in school and there is nothing special about me. Sometimes it makes me wish they'd fail at something, just so I wouldn't feel like such a loser. Is that breaking the commandment about coveting?*

Bless your heart. Yeah, it is. But you don't have to keep doing it. Although changing the way you feel is going to take some time, there are some things you can do. For starters, pray, pray, pray about feeling not as good as the others. Ask God to help you replace those thoughts with the truth, which is that God loves you and made you every bit as pretty and smart and talented as your friends in ways you haven't even discovered yet.

Start looking for what shines in you. Make a list of the things you do well, down to the teeniest. Do you make a mean platter of nachos? Is your room adorable because you're so good at decorating? Do you have a contagious laugh that seems to make other people laugh with you? Are you always the first in your group of Girlz to know who's down or upset? Develop those wonderful talents and qualities in yourself. Go back to the "I'm Not Worthy!" chapter and use some of the things on the list you just made as your goals. Learn to make more kinds of Mexican dishes. Redecorate the Girlz Only Clubhouse. Keep a journal. That chapter will help you achieve those goals. You'll be so busy working on your own stuff, you'll think less about how much better you think everybody else is—and you sure won't wish they'd fail, because you'll be succeeding!

✿ *SUZY: My sister and my mom are really close and I feel so left out sometimes. The other day I got so sick of it, I told my mom that my sister kissed a boy in the back seat of the bus on the way home. She did, so I wasn't lying. But I feel bad now that I got my sister in trouble. I just don't know why.*

You feel bad because your **motivation** was wrong. Motivation is the answer to the question: why did you do it? Did you tell your mom your sister was kissing some boy on the bus because you were concerned about your sister and wanted to make sure your mom is able to steer her in the right direction? I don't think so. You know that your real reason for telling on her was to get her into trouble—because you're envious of her relationship with your mom. If your mom can see that your sister isn't perfect, maybe that'll mess up what they have and make more room for you, right? Well, wrong.

It's never okay to try to manipulate (change around) somebody else's relationship. It would be so much better for you to try to have your own relationship with your mom. Try to figure out what you two have in common and then ask your mom to join you in one of those things. Do you both love ice cream? Save up some money and ask her if you can treat her to an ice cream sundae one afternoon. Are you both into old Shirley Temple movies? Pop some popcorn into the microwave and offer to put her feet up for her while you both watch one on television. Go to your mom with your problems—maybe even this one. Tell her about the good stuff that's happening in your life. Could it be that the reason your sister is so close to your mom is because she does these very things?

Just Do It

Let's see how you do with commandments eight ("You shall not steal") and ten ("You shall not covet . . . anything that belongs to your neighbor"). (See Deuteronomy 5:7–21 for a list of the Ten Commandments.)

Which of the statements below (or something close to it) have you heard most often inside your own head? Put a star beside it.

_____ "If somebody is careless enough to leave their paper uncovered, it's *their* fault if I copy an answer."

_____ "Finders keepers, losers weepers."

_____ "I don't like her—she's a teacher's pet."

_____ "She just thinks she's all that. If my parents had as much money as her parents do, I could have all that stuff too."

_____ "What's so good about that? I could do as well if I wanted to."

_____ "I should have won. It's no fair. I hope her trophy falls on her head."

_____ "I might not be as smart as he is, but at least I'm not a geek."

_____ "Who cares if she got it? I really didn't want it anyway."

_____ "I wish I had one of those."

On a piece of paper or a card, write that starred sentence down. Now put a big X over it. Below it, write a sentence you could replace it with, one that follows the commandments about loving God with everything you've got and loving your neighbor as yourself. Use one of the statements below or create your own.

- Taking someone else's answers is always cheating. Cheating is stealing. Study instead!
- It belongs to someone else. It isn't yours just because you found it. What you need to find now is the owner!
- If the teacher likes her so much, maybe I will too. I'll get to know her.

My parents don't have a lot of money, but I sure appreciate what they do buy for me. I'm so lucky.

- It must be neat to be that good at something. I think I'll work at it too.
- I'm bummed that I didn't win this time. I'll try harder for next time.
- Everybody has a gift. I enjoy mine, and I love it that everybody else has one too!
- If you really want something, work for it. If you can't work for it, pray about it. If God says no, forget about it. It wasn't meant to be.
- God—help! This jealousy, envy, coveting thing is tearing me up!

Whenever that X'd out sentence pops into your head, take out one of these replacement sentences or think up one of your own. Say it to yourself like a prayer. After a while, it's going to take the place of that jealous, envious, covetous thought that used to eat you up. It's going to take time and work, but don't give up. And remember—most of all, it's going to take God.

Talking to God About It

Dear _____ (your favorite way of addressing our Lord),

As you know, I'm having trouble with some of these things:

_____ Cheating

_____ Keeping things that don't really belong to me

_____ Wishing I had what other people have

_____ Disliking people because I think they're better than I am

_____ Hoping bad stuff will happen to somebody who got what I wanted

_____ Saying nasty things (sometimes even true) to or about people I'm jealous of

_____ Pretending I don't care when I lose and somebody else wins

_____ Doing whatever I can to win, even if it doesn't follow the commandments

Would you please help me to yank those things right out of myself and guide me in replacing them with what's real and good—love for you and love for my neighbors and love for myself?

I know I can start by thanking you for all that you have given me: For all the things I own that I treasure

_____

_____

For the people in my life who love me

_____

_____

For the gifts and talents that make me who I am

_____

_____

For the blessings in my life that make me secure and happy

_____

_____

For my relationship with you, God, that makes me feel so

_____

_____

With all of that, Lord, why would I want a single thing that some-one else has? Please help me never to forget that, but to concentrate on developing the gifts you have given me. Help me to support other people as they find theirs, especially _____.

I love you.

The good things I wish for the person I'm most envious of are . . .

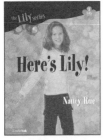

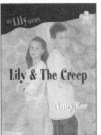
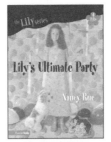
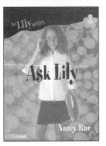

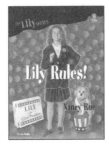

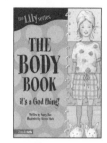

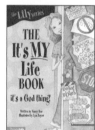

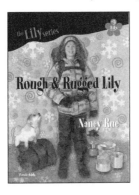
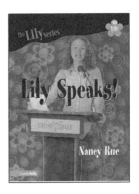

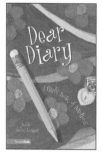
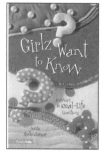

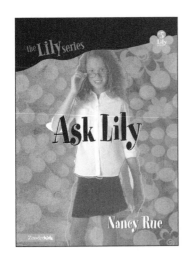

If you liked *The Blurry Rules Book,* you'll love its fictional companion book *Ask Lily!*

L ily, come *on!* We're gonna be late!"

"I can't get this stupid locker open!"

"We're gonna get in trouble—you heard what Mrs. Reinhold said—"

Lily blew her mop of red hair out of her face and attacked the lock again. "Yeah, Reni," she said. "If we come to class without our literature books we're chopped meat. Do you remember my combination?"

"I can't even remember *mine!*" Reni glanced over her shoulder at the last of the kids streaming out of the locker area toward their classrooms. "We're gonna get busted for being late, and Mr. Lamb's gonna hear about it, and that's gonna go against me making All-State Orchestra."

Lily gave the lock another vicious twist, and the locker door popped open. *Adventures in World Literature* tumbled out onto her foot.

Reni snatched it up and made off for D–104. Still wincing, Lily slammed the locker door, slung her backpack (which was still gaping open) over her shoulder, and limped after Reni.

You're going to like middle school so much more than elementary, Lily, Ms. Gooch, her sixth-grade teacher, had told her at the end of last year.

"Oh, yeah, I adore it," she muttered to herself as she hobbled the last few steps to her classroom. There were two different locker combinations to remember—PE *and* a book locker—and seven different teachers' rules to follow—*plus* the nine *hundred* rules Cedar Hills Middle School had on its list.

Even now, she realized she was walking on the wrong side of the hallway, and she had to swerve abruptly to get back to where she was supposed to be. Bad move. Three binders escaped from the unzipped backpack and dumped themselves and their contents in an arc across the floor. Last night's English homework made a beeline for the area right under the water fountain, where it soaked up the remains of someone's drink. Ink from Lily's purple gel pen oozed sickeningly down the paper.

Reni turned from the classroom doorway, her brown eyes popping wide.

"Oh, no, you did *not!*" she said.

"Look at my homework!" Lily said. "I am so busted!"

Reni let her own backpack fall with a thud and dove for Lily's math binder that was splayed out near the trash can.

"No—get to class!" Lily said. "No point in both of us getting in trouble."

But the bell rang before Reni could answer, and a shadow fell over them from the doorway. It was Mrs. Reinhold.

"We're not late," Reni said to her, scrambling up with the last of Lily's belongings in both hands. "Lily dumped her backpack."

"I can see that," Mrs. Reinhold said.

She adjusted her almost-too-tiny-for-her-eyes glasses with the tips of both index fingers, as if she wanted to get a better focus on Lily, who was now using two arms to hug her backpack against her chest. Its contents poked out like yesterday's recycling pile.

Haven't you ever seen anybody spaz out before? Lily wanted to say to her. She was sure Mrs. Reinhold had. She'd probably been a seventh-grade English teacher since Noah was in middle school, and she'd definitely brought her disciplinary methods with her off the ark. Right now she was directing her pointed nose at Lily and frowning.

"If you had given yourself less time for visiting and more time for getting to class, Liliana, this wouldn't have happened," Mrs. Reinhold said in the voice that always reminded Lily of cobwebs.

"Are you gonna mark us tardy?" Reni said.

"'Gonna'?" Mrs. Reinhold said. "I'm not familiar with the word 'gonna.'"

Lily pulled her full lips into the biggest smile she could muster in the face of fear and slipped past Mrs. Reinhold toward her desk in the first row by the door. At least she didn't have to parade her trash heap of a backpack in front of the whole class. But Chelsea Gordon was sitting in Lily's seat and curling her lip at her as if Lily had yet again proven herself to be the biggest geek on the planet.

"Liliana, you are now in the far row," Mrs. Reinhold's cobweb voice rang out behind her. "I've done some rearranging to eliminate the visiting that has been transpiring."

Lily's heart sank as her eyes moved in the direction the teacher was pointing. Ashley Adamson, Chelsea's best friend and closest clone, was sitting in front of Lily's new desk. No one could make Lily feel more like she'd just graduated from Un-cool School with high honors than Ashley.

Pick up a copy today at your local bookstore!

Softcover 0-310-23254-6

We want to hear from you. Please send your comments about this book to us in care of the address below. Thank you.

Grand Rapids, MI 49530
www.zonderkidz.com